GW01003280

THE AUTHORITY GUIDE TO
NETWORKING FOR
BUSINESS GROWTH

How to master confident, effective networking
and win more business

ROB BROWN

The Authority Guide to Networking for Business Growth

How to master confident, effective networking and win more business

© Rob Brown

ISBN 978-1-909116-98-6

eISBN 978-1-912300-00-6

Published in 2017 by Authority Guides

authorityguides.co.uk

The right of Rob Brown to be identified as the author
of this work has been asserted by him in accordance with the
Copyright, Designs and Patents Act 1988.

A CIP record of this book is available from the British Library.

Printed in the United Kingdom.

Acknowledgements

It's generally easy to do the small stuff, but big projects like this need a team. This means there are always people to thank when you finally get over the line.

I've thanked, blessed, acknowledged and shouted out plenty of people personally for their help and encouragement over the years. Specifically, my best friend and wife, Amanda, who always gets huge credit for keeping my life, family and business going while I do the sexy stuff like writing and speaking.

My mum will be proud. She has always encouraged my writing, so thanks, Mum. My pastors, Kate, Ali and John, deserve thanks for investing in me over the years. Still a work in progress, but further on than I was in faith and character. My in-laws, Dawn and Stu, have likewise been hugely generous, supporting and believing from the outset.

I'm blessed to be in two amazing mastermind groups, so big thanks to the guys in Catalyst and Gauntlet for their support, critical eye and brilliant ideas. You have put me through it and brought me out the other side.

Throughout my recovery from brain surgery in 2016, I'm indebted both to friends I knew would be alongside me and to friends I didn't know I had. Thanks for the walks, the visits, the encouragement, the uplifting prayers and practical help that got me back to somewhere near my best.

Thanks to Oliver and Phoebe, my grad students who helped with editing and research, and generally kept things going in the business while delivered on the deadlines.

My two incredible daughters, Georgia and Madison, get much credit for their wise words, coaching, appreciation, love and humour, which keep me going.

Finally, my God, the alpha and the omega, the source of all goodness and strength, thank you, Lord.

Contents

Contents

Introduction

Networking has existed since the dawn of time. Ever since humans started communicating with people they don't know, we've had networking. Back in the day, people would tell you that it's all about 'who you know'. But somewhere along the way, networking got commercialised. Named and claimed. Hijacked and highlighted. And largely for good reason.

Connecting and being connected is a route to the top, whatever the top looks like for you. Your network says much about you. It accounts for many of the opportunities that come your way. People even say that your income will be the average of that of the five business people you most associate with.

So investing in mastering the skill of business networking is a smart move. This might be the only education you get on the topic apart from the odd blog post or wise word from a seasoned rainmaker. So buckle up, get your business cards printed and let's get ready to network!

How good a networker are you?

This is the perfect question to start with. It gives you a benchmark, a starting point. You've probably never been taught how to network. At best, you've sat through a workshop or read a few articles. Maybe you've watched a few people in action who you consider to be good at the networking thing.

A great first task is to take the Networking Success Test. Go to networkingsuccesstest.com and spend five minutes answering the questions. It quizzes you on the eight core competencies of networking, from the mindset and preparation to the execution, dialogue and follow-through. Your score will be a percentage, and you'll see how you compare to the world's best (and worst) networkers. For the moment, the test is free.

Great networkers are made as well as born. What's for certain is that we can all improve. The skills of networking are coachable. There are two main skill sets in networking. First, the sexy, social working the room and chatting stuff. Then, the unsexy, disciplined and organised follow-up. Few people love them both, but both need to be done to make money from networking.

Do you struggle to make networking work?

Do you want more sales, more leads and more business from your networking efforts? If you've got any kind of sales, marketing or business-development angle to your role, then you'll recognise how vital networking and referrals can be in your lead generation. The trouble is, few people know how to do it properly. As a result, they get frustrated or worn down by networking and connecting. Do you recognise any of these problems?

- Wanting and needing to network but not knowing quite where to start.

- Moving into a new role or location with few useful contacts you can leverage.

- Struggling to break into established networks where everyone seems to know each other.

- Wanting referrals but not having a big enough network or client base to get them from.
- Getting into good networking situations but not knowing how to start meaningful conversations.
- Struggling to reach your target market through traditional networking events.
- Returning from networking events with a pocketful of business cards that are of no use to you.
- Coming back with lots of business cards but not knowing how to turn them into business.

If these sound familiar, you're not alone. Most people struggle with making networking work. When you're not confident or particularly effective with your networking, you're not going to get tangible results, which is a shame, because as a route to market and a way to uncover new business opportunities, networking works. This failure to get results is not because many people don't know how to generate return on investment (ROI) from networking, it's because they ignore it entirely.

Can you ignore networking?

Where does your business come from? When asked, most people say referrals, recommendations, introductions, repeat business. Think about this. All of that stuff comes from relationships and connections. You've got to know people to capitalise on those lead sources.

That means some kind of marketing, outreach or networking. If you ignore networking, you're left with other perhaps more expensive and often less productive avenues of lead generation, such as cold-calling, email marketing, advertising, PR and direct mail.

Of course, you can ignore networking but, if you're responsible for winning new business, you ignore it at your peril. You're in a people business. You're in a relationship business. Referrals come from people. So does repeat business. And the best way to develop a network of fresh, influential introducers and potential new clients is by getting out there, shaking their hands and having a meaningful conversation.

This is what networking is. Trouble is, if you're like most people, you're probably not comfortable with networking. Good news, though – that's not your fault.

It's not your fault

Networking is a critical skill for business. Knowing and being known by the right people opens doors to new deals, investors, customers, clients, mentors, staff, partners, buyers and experts. Yet, very few people claim to feel comfortable, competent or enthusiastic when it comes to networking.

Why is this? One reason is that skills such as networking are rarely taught. They're not part of any university curriculum, commercial qualification or on-the-job accreditation. Nobody really teaches you how to work a room and move a conversation from small talk to business talk. You will never be shown how to introduce and position yourself properly when meeting people and how to handle the conversation to create opportunities. Little training is ever given on how to follow up your contacts, keep in touch and turn them into business.

So, if you're not particularly confident or effective when it comes to networking, it's not your fault. However, it is your responsibility. Investing in networking and relationships eats into your most precious commodity – time. It's time away from your inbox, your family, your golf game, your gym class, your friends and your existing clients.

You've probably realised that's my story. I learned the hard way. For you, it will be much easier, much faster and much more enjoyable, because you have this book in your hand. Networking is a brilliant way to raise your profile, source new referral partners and meet new clients.

A typical networking story

Once upon a time, a talented, handsome young man left a promising career in teaching to seek his fortune in the world of sales. His new company gave him 75 per cent of his leads, meaning he had to generate 25 per cent on his own. Having all the product knowledge in the world but no clue how to actually generate business, he was initially at a loss what to do. Then his boss suggested he try networking: *'You'll like networking because you dress up, you go out, you meet some nice people, you shake some hands, you swap some cards, you drink some nice drinks and you eat some nice food. It's like partying but without the dancing!'*

So off he went with his box of brand-new business cards to every networking event he could find. Trouble was, he had no idea what he was doing. Two years later, he'd attended 126 events and spent thousands on breakfasts, lunches, dinners, mixers, conferences, group memberships and club subscriptions. And secured exactly *zero* business. Nobody told him that you go networking to make money, not spend money.

In these two years, he'd wasted precious hours and precious money and won no work. All he had to show for his efforts was the 2,987 business cards he'd collected. He felt like he was doing everything right but, in reality, he was a brilliant example of how *not* to network. He could count his conversations, but not make his conversations count.

Learning to think differently

He was faced with a return to teaching or somehow becoming a more confident and effective networker. He chose the latter, got some education and training, watched what the good networkers were doing and took some action. In just 13 months, he'd multiplied the small amount of business he was generating from the company leads by a factor of 15! That's when people began to take notice of what he was doing and asked for help in doing the same. And a new career was born – ever since then, he's been teaching people how to network successfully.

In this book, you have everything you need to begin making networking work to generate more leads, sales and business. For you, that means you hit your targets, keep your boss off your back and keep your bank balance full. Let's get started.

How to use this book

You should be able to read this whole book in two hours. If you have a short attention span, it's broken down for you into three parts explaining what to do:

1. Before you go networking: mindset, strategy and preparation

2. While you're there networking: working a room, handling the dialogue

3. After you've been networking: following up, keeping in touch

Some people will use this book as a resource to dip into for particular situations or scenarios. Others will read it to get a thorough grounding in what it takes to make money from networking. If you're really pushed for time, each part has a brief summary entitled 'Key takeaways'. These are your action points which distil the core messages into short soundbites and key lessons.

Let's talk about customers and clients for a moment. They mean the same things to most people. It's simply those who buy from you. I prefer the word 'client' and use it throughout the book. Client is a more relational word. Customer to me is a transactional word. I work a lot with accountants and lawyers, who use client rather than customer. I also work a lot with bankers, who use customer. Whatever works. Client works for me so substitute your own word when you see it – buyers, patrons, investors, supporters…

A final point before we get moving. Networking is a process as much as an event. It's more like a long-term relationship than a one-night stand. So make the commitment to invest in networking like you invest in any relationship or marketing activity. It involves some heavy lifting and intentional effort to get things moving.

Key takeaways

- Networking, if done well, is a powerful way to source new business and raise your profile.

- Networking is generally not taught, so it's up to you to teach and coach yourself.

- Networking is coachable – everyone can learn how to do it. Networkers are born *and* made. If you think a little differently about it, you can make it work for you.

- Networking represents precious time away from important stuff like your inbox, your family and your personal time. So make it work for you.

- There is no one networking style or one-size-fits-all strategy. Follow your own path according to your own personality, strengths and objectives.

- Don't count your conversations, but make your conversations count.

- Prospecting is vital for sales. Without networking, you're relying on avenues like cold-calling and email marketing.

You can't afford to be a well-kept secret. The business, the deal, the sale, the contract goes to those who are known to potential buyers and introducers as the obvious choice and stand-out voice for what they do. You're about to discover how networking will help you do that.

Part I
Before you go

Your richest resources will always be found in your richest relationships. Almost every deal, sale and transaction comes down to two people shaking hands. And networking is the ultimate way to source, engage and leverage those connections that will build your reputation, your business and your bank balance.

But before you attend any kind of networking event, let's get you fit and ready to exploit the situation. In this part, we'll get your mindset straight so your networking attitude is positive. We'll get your strategy exact, so you show up in the right places having the right conversations with the right people. And we'll get your preparation right, so you make the most of every event you attend.

Networking is people looking for people looking for people.

Jarod Kintz

1. What is business networking?

Business networking is often misunderstood. Ask 20 people exactly what it is and you'll get 21 different answers. So let's clarify by starting with some definitions. Networking is all of these:

- Talking and listening – things you've been doing since you were young.

- Sourcing and building the right relationships with the right people.

- Creating a network of valuable contacts that will accelerate your commercial objectives.

- Creating introducers, advocates and champions to enhance your reputation.

- Building and leveraging high-level connections for career advancement.

- Getting on to the radars of the right people so you become the go-to choice.

- Strategically assembling an army of introducers who will refer you work and opportunities.

- Shaking hands, meeting people and turning strangers into friends.

- Asking questions which lead to good conversations and good relationships.
- Knowing and being known by sufficient numbers of the right people.

Bottom line, networking has two aspects. First is the act of networking, a function-based definition. This is attending social and business events to fulfil your commercial objectives. Second is the activity of networking, a process-based definition. This is building your professional and personal network strategically over time. When you do the first, you get the second. Both are networking, and both are vital pieces of your sales jigsaw.

What networking isn't

- Networking isn't a dark art or mysterious science. It's basically common sense. It's emotional intelligence – getting on with people and having conversations. Everyone can do that – there's no exclusivity, secret code or barrier to entry.

- Networking isn't a closed private club or old boys' network. Not any more. Anyone can start a networking group or club. Anyone can start a conversation. If you can say hello and goodbye, you're in the club!

- Networking isn't just face to face. Social media and the Internet have changed all that. You can network any time and any place with practically anyone if you have a mobile phone or an Internet connection.

- Networking isn't selling. Of course, you're selling yourself but, ultimately, networking gives you the platform to sell in the future. It kickstarts the sales conversation but doesn't make the sale.

- Networking isn't counting cards. It's not a numbers game and it's not a mass-marketing activity like email. It's building relationships one conversation at a time.

- Networking is not a one-time performance. It's not really a dip-in and dip-out sport. Business is not won by the casual networker who parachutes into an event, sprays their business cards around and walks away with big deals. If you're going to do it that way, you've got to rely on luck and timing to get anywhere. You've got to be talking to exactly the right person with exactly the right need and exactly the right budget at exactly the right time. How likely is that?

In short, networking is a blend of short-term conversations and long-term relationship building. And when you get it right, there are many benefits.

To succeed in this world you have to be known to people. The alternative is obscurity.

Sonia Sotomayor

2. Why is networking important, especially for sales?

There are many benefits for the diligent and consistent networker. If you have to win business and bring in clients, networking is a great way to do it. If you do it right, you are guaranteed to enjoy these many networking benefits:

- **More opportunities.** The more you're out there, the more doors you will open, conversations you will have and needs you will uncover.
- **More clients.** Your prospects are out there networking, whether at face-to-face business-related events or social functions or on online platforms. Networking is a great way to reach them.
- **Met and exceeded targets.** Hitting targets, making plans or meeting quotas is a constant pressure. Networking generates leads, establishes introducers and raises your profile as the ultimate choice for what you do.
- **More profits.** With more revenue comes more profits. Once you build a relationship, invest in a new referral source or win a client, it's all extra profit from there. You don't have to spend much more to win that business.

- **Easier marketing.** Marketing is noise. You're trying to shout louder than the others. Face-to-face networking builds high trust, quick rapport and long-term relationships. It's got to be easier than cold-calling or paid advertising.

- **Greater choice.** If you've got good business coming in, a healthy pipeline and a strong network of referral sources, you can say no to stuff you don't want. That's a wonderful position of choice to be in.

- **More ongoing work.** Lifetime client value means new business isn't just a transaction. If you look after them, there should be all kinds of cross-sales, up-sales and repeat work coming your way.

- **More referrals.** Existing clients are a great source of referrals. Your professional network and wider contacts are great sources of referrals. Build this network and you'll generate much more referral business.

- **Greater reputation.** You want to get on the radars of the right people. Remember your network is who you know and your reputation is who knows you. One builds the other!

- **Quicker growth.** Growth comes when you know and are known by the right people. That means your target market, your introducer base, your wider network. When they bring you business, growth is always faster.

And we haven't even mentioned the support, encouragement, ideas, market insight, profile, friendships and career openings that come from networking.

3. How do you approach networking positively?

Networking is a process, not an event

One of the best ways to overcome any networking reticence is to look at networking in a different and more healthy way. Rather than seeing networking as a conversation or an event, think more strategically. Turning networking into sales, and conversations into contracts, has five distinct phases:

1. **Mindset.** Start with a good, open and expectant attitude.

2. **Strategy.** Plan your approach so you network with the right people.

3. **Execution.** Master the talking and working the room.

4. **Follow-up.** Stay connected and keep in touch until they need you.

5. **Convert.** Sell yourself well, then sell your product or service well.

Combatting your networking fears

If you're like most people, networking is probably one of your biggest fears. You know you've got to do it. You know it's important, but the thought of meeting strangers, walking into a room full of dark suits... this arouses feelings of anxiety, stress, worry, discomfort and even fear in pretty much everyone.

You already know that networking is simply talking and listening. It's shaking hands and meeting new people. And ever since you were born, you've been communicating. You've been meeting strangers and you've been making an impact. You started out fearlessly talking to anyone, any time, any place. It's just that somewhere along the line, you lost your mojo, your hunger, your skills.

4. How does psychology and motivation play a part?

What's your networking mindset?

Networking is as much a mindset as an activity. It's creating a series of *value-for-value exchanges*. When your attitude is good, your behaviour and confidence will follow. Calibrate your thinking about networking before you even accept an invitation and you'll accelerate your results significantly. Some pointers:

- **Think help as well as sell.** People say that when you give, you gain, and this is true. But you must also keep in mind your own commercial objectives. You can go broke helping other people, so keep it balanced. Transactional networkers aim to get before they give. Be more relational.

- **Think quality *and* quantity.** A good network is deep and wide, diverse and niched. It's a combination of numbers and strength. With the tools, apps and technology around today, it's much easier to manage a large network of contacts.

- **Keep it real.** Authenticity sells, so be genuine in your interactions. People can spot fakes a mile off. Be genuinely interested in others. This can be hard if you're lacking empathy or you're a hard-nosed task-driven person. People love being liked, appreciated and valued. So be yourself and take an interest in others, and you'll find good things come back to you.

- **Start with who you know.** Many people make the mistake of going out looking for new connections and ignoring their existing ones. Don't neglect the business cards you already have and the people you already know. Without even going to an event, you should consider reaching out by phone, email or social media to your existing network.

- **Think long term.** Networking gives you slow burns and quick wins. Sometimes the timing is perfect and you can win business quickly. Other times you are merely the right idea at the wrong moment. So be patient and play a long-term game.

- **Be expectant.** Perhaps you've been scarred by networking or had a bad experience. But you've got to walk into that room expecting good things. People are inherently good. If you're distrustful, suspicious or moody, you'll attract the same kind of people. So be positive and expectant, then hopefully you'll get the same back.

- **Be open.** If you're seeing networking as boring endless chats to people you don't like, or crammed rooms of people throwing business cards at each other, you'll never embrace networking. Be open to meeting interesting people, learning interesting things and developing interesting relationships.

You need to get your mindset and attitude right for networking, and everything else will follow. Let's quickly explore another aspect of networking mindset – your motivation.

Getting motivated to network

How much do you want to network? What's driving you? If you don't have a desire to do it, you're probably not going to make it work. Networking under duress is not a nice place to be. You've got to find your reason why. We all have different reasons for networking. Do any of these personal wins appeal to you?

- Placing yourself prominently in the minds of the right people.
- Keeping yourself prominently in the minds of the right people.
- Developing you and your network for now and for the future.
- Connecting for company, camaraderie and community.
- Doing it because you're told to and have to – or else!
- Fulfilling a sense of professionalism, pride and duty.

Networking will deliver all these wins if you do it right. What about these business wins?

- Sourcing and winning new business, and cross-/up-selling old business.
- Educating markets on new initiatives, products and services.
- Courting suitable players and prospects at particular events.
- Defending existing contacts and clients from competitors.
- Finding great suppliers, advisors, mentors, providers and experts.
- Making your mark in a new sector, role or geographical area.

These drivers begin to form your 'reason why' – your specific objectives for networking. What is your 'reason why' for networking? Make a declaration of intent right here on your motivation for networking. Take a moment to write down what your pay-offs, upsides or key benefits are to becoming a more confident and effective networker. It's probably going to be about more business and a higher profile with your target audience.

You'll need to own this statement – it will drive you forward in your moments of weakness.

Now that you have got your mindset and your motivation sorted, you can begin devising your networking strategy.

5. What are the different ways to network?

As you'll see on page 29, there are seven different approaches to networking and meeting the people you want to meet. There is no one way to network. It's a fallacy that networkers are born, not made. Different people do it in different ways. Your approach will depend on the following six factors:

1 **Your personal strengths**. Everybody's different. You have a unique blend of talents, abilities, communication styles and traits. Your strengths are not my strengths. Your weapons are not my weapons. There are some things you will be naturally good at that I might find really difficult, and vice versa. Playing to your strengths means you get results more quickly and more naturally.

2 **Your personality type**. Introverts actually make great networkers because they talk less, listen more and generally ask good questions that make other people talk. But obviously the way you're wired up will affect your ability to get the most out of certain networking situations. For instance, if you're better in one-to-one situations than in crowds, you can network accordingly.

3 **Your current network**. If you've already got a great network, you probably don't need to meet too many

new people. Your strategy should focus on developing those relationships you already have for more referrals and possibly more prospects. Alternatively, if you have a good network but they are not the kind of people you need, then you certainly will need to go out and make new connections.

④ **Your target audience**. Who you want to connect with and talk to plays a big part in your networking strategy. You've got to fish where the fish you want to catch are swimming. It's no good turning up for weekly business breakfasts if your prospects are attending black-tie dinners and conferences. Go where they go for best results.

⑤ **Your availability**. If you have ten hours to network in a week, your approach will be different than if you only have one hour. Your strategy will depend on how busy you are and how much time you can devote to networking. Obviously, some strategies are more time consuming than others. For instance, attending an industry conference may take two days, while reaching out to somebody on LinkedIn may take only two minutes.

⑥ **Your objectives**. What's driving you to network? Your needs and objectives are possibly not mine. You've already looked at your motivators and drivers. These are the reasons why you network. They represent your objectives in building and executing your networking strategy.

You're laying the foundations for networking success. You are not just blindly showing up to business events, throwing your cards around and hoping something good happens. Before you actually go out there and execute, let's look at the key elements of a successful networking strategy.

6. How do you plan a successful networking strategy?

Who do you want to network with?

Knowing who you sell to and who you want to meet are good starting points for your networking journey. When you know what your best customer or client looks like, you can go looking for them. Networking pros know their target market or niche. You can find anybody if you know what they look like and where they hang out. There are two ways to do this:

1. **Network *to* the room.** Do this when you have direct access to a room or website full of your kind of prospects. If they attend certain events or show up on certain online networks, then that's where you need to be.

   Look for: end users, consumers, potential customers – the kind of fish you want to swim with.

2. **Network *through* the room.** Do this when you cannot easily and directly reach your prospects, but you see people who can. Go through the people around you – they can *connect* you to your target market.

Look for: the suppliers, advisors, providers, customers, contacts and clients of your perfect prospect. Plus potential introducers, intermediaries, connectors and door openers that move around and have influence with your target market.

Where do your targets network?

Once you've figured out your networking targets, think where you're going to find them so you can get an invitation to the party. You can reach people through any thousands of networking groups, clubs, organisations, associations, platforms, social networks and online directories, but you neither have the time nor energy to be everywhere. Nor do you need to be. You've got to play where your prospects play.

Focus is vital with networking. The right networking strategy means you go to the right events and have the right conversations with the right people for the right mutually beneficial outcomes. Your networking might take place online using social media and platforms like LinkedIn, or it might be face to face at the many networking groups, clubs and affiliations that will bring you into the same room as your prospects or connectors. You might do both as the good networkers do.

Let's look at the different approaches to networking. These are characterised by where you do it – the various kinds of networking opportunities available to you.

The seven networking approaches

There are really only seven ways to build your network. Seven approaches, seven kinds of networking situations where you can meet new people to further your commercial objectives. The matrix on the next page shows them all. As you move from left to right, you'll notice that you have increasing control over the encounter.

Figure 1 Matrix of the seven approaches to networking

Control means you have the power to decide who is in the conversation, where and when it happens, and if it happens at all. Increased commitment on the left-hand side reflects the amount of time and effort you'll need to put into that approach to make it work.

As you go through these, think about those factors that affect your networking strategy. Again, these are your strengths, your personality, your current network, your target audience, your availability, your own objectives and your motivations. You want a primary 'route to market' as well as a secondary one upon which you'll focus most of your networking efforts.

1. **ONE (one-off networking events).** Think of functions that are annual. Big-signature events that take place just once a year. They are prestigious, exclusive and generally feature

a good range of senior decision makers, influencers, big hitters and leaders. Examples: black-tie awards dinners, trade shows, exhibitions, conferences, special seminars, hospitality functions and major sporting events.

2 **Loose.** These are usually monthly and involve some kind of membership. Because they are regular, you'll find the attendees are more about building relationships than being seen. There is usually a good mix of entrepreneurial and professional people. Examples: Chamber of Commerce, Institute of Directors (IoD), professional and trade associations, local networking groups and clubs.

3 **Strong.** These tend to meet weekly, with the main focus on generating referrals for members, so you'll probably have to pay to join. Often (but not always) key sectors, trades and professions are allocated, meaning there is one accountant, one banker, one lawyer, one IT specialist and so on. The sentiment is high trust and regular attendance, hence the highest level of commitment. Examples: BNI, 4Networking and a range of local networking groups and clubs that meet weekly or fortnightly.

4 **Social.** Moving to the right, this approach fits into the nooks and crannies of your life. So it doesn't involve specific events, but rather chances to have conversations and meet people while you're doing other things. You can start chatting to people almost anywhere, and who knows what might come of those courageous first moves? Examples: sports, hobbies, leisure (trips, tourist stuff, walking your dog, ramblers), transport (chats on trains, planes, buses, waiting lounges, queues) and children-related (picking up your kids from school, watching them play sports).

(5) **Online.** The networking landscape has changed over recent years. Traditionally, networking was done face to face. Now we have social media and a range of online networking platforms where you can source new contacts and build relationships. Examples: LinkedIn, Twitter and Facebook.

(6) **SHE (self-hosted events).** This is where you bring the world to you. You set the theme, you choose the venue, you dictate the guest list, you send out the invitations and you run the event. You can use platforms like Eventbrite to handle bookings and any payments for you. There are so many ways now to promote an event and put people on seats. Examples: seminars, forums, client-appreciation evenings, private dinners and joint events with others.

(7) **LEN (leveraging existing networks).** When you already have plenty of business cards, contacts and relationships, then this is a good strategy. You focus on who you already know and aim to deepen the relationships with them rather than go after new people. Examples: customer relationship management (CRM) databases, contact lists, introducers, prospects, influencers and existing clients.

Why networking isn't selling

Most people have been on the receiving end of the enthusiastic networker handing round business cards, bragging about their offering and making unsolicited pitches in full-on sales mode. It's not attractive and certainly not effective. It's said that networking and selling are like oil and water. They both belong in your financial engine, but you put them in separate containers.

The best way to look at selling from a networking perspective is to see your approach as a series of stages rather than a one-off pitch. Start by sourcing or finding the kind of people you want to connect with. Then start communicating with them, talking to them, asking them good questions. Now you're moving into the realm of investing in people to build those relationships. Only now are you in a position to present what you do to more receptive ears.

Dr Ivan Misner, founder of the world's largest networking organisation BNI, puts this elegantly in three words: VISIBILITY–CREDIBILITY–PROFITABLILTY. First, you've got to be seen and acknowledged. Then you've got to be accepted and trusted. Only then will the sales, the introductions and referrals come.

Of course, the one thing you are selling is yourself. Only once they've bought you can you begin to position what you do and how you might help them. In fact, the words 'sell' and 'help' are similar in some respects, but there's a subtle difference. Bottom line – turn back the dial on being pushy and overbearing. Talk less, listen more and ask good questions. Which ironically is what the very best sales people do. Remember, networking is not selling but, if done well, it gives you the opportunity to sell down the line.

You're now just about ready to go out networking. You've begun to formulate your strategy and you've got an approach that plays to your strengths, answers your 'reason why' and delivers on your objectives. Let's begin to put it all together so you can make your next networking experience a successful one.

Setting the right networking goals

You're not quite ready to walk into a room full of strangers, but you're close. You can't afford to run the risk of just showing up to a business-related event hoping something good will happen. You must be more focused than that. The best networkers usually are. They do things for a reason. They are strategic and intentional. They go with a purpose.

Likewise, when you attend business-related meetings or engage with people online, you should be purposeful. That means having an outcome in mind. Otherwise, you're just talking and not being strategic about your networking. Here are some examples of possible networking goals or objectives that you could aim to accomplish at a particular event. Obviously, you won't use all of them at every event, but certainly one or two. If you use these, you'll ensure you don't just count your conversations, you'll make your conversations count.

- To collect X number of business cards.

- To hand out five business cards.

- To have, say, three meaningful conversations.

- To meet, say, two quality prospects.

- To uncover X number of new introducers or potential referral sources.

- To create X number of new partnerships or business opportunities.

- To practise a particular networking skill. This could be your elevator pitch, your questioning techniques or your working-the-room skills.

- To learn two new pieces of information or gossip.

- To conquer a specific fear. This could be approaching strangers, remembering names or making introductions.
- To have a conversation with a particular person. This could be someone you've decided in advance you'd like to meet, a VIP or even the speaker at your event.

Great networkers value their time and make each event and each interaction count for something. Even if it's just eliminating some people, it's all about having conversations with more of the right people to fulfil your business goals. So be focused with your networking and create one or two objectives for every business-related event you attend. This will increase the likelihood that your networking efforts will result in business and sales down the road. Unless you're there to wander aimlessly, talking to all the wrong people, go with a goal. This is your precious time, so make it count.

Key takeaways

Like an iceberg, much of the work that goes into networking is below the surface – done before you even walk in the room. Mindset, preparation, strategy – they all count in getting you to the right kind of networking events. Only then will you have the right conversations with the right people. Here's a summary of the key takeaways from this section:

- Networking is simply talking and listening to build relationships and create opportunities. You've been doing it forever, so don't stop now.
- Most people feel anxious about networking, even the most extrovert leaders. It's normal. You get over your fears by working on your strategy, your motivations, your skills and your scripts so you know what to do.

- Everyone can be a confident and effective networker, introverts included. You just have to do it in a way that plays to your personality, strengths and particular objectives.

- Networking brings huge benefits for anyone with a sales role. You raise your profile and fill your pipeline with good prospects. You also generate referrals through introducers who can get you to your target market.

- See networking as a process or series of phases, rather than an event. Get your mindset and strategy right, and you'll be ready to execute and follow up, then convert and sell.

- The more clearly you can articulate what kind of people you want to meet, the more likely you'll end up in the same room as them having good conversations.

- There are seven approaches to networking. All are valid and all work. But to be successful, you've got to choose the best ones for you and your unique situation.

- Networking isn't selling. It gives you the foundation to sell at a future date. Think *help* rather than *sell* and you'll do okay.

Networking fails when people fail. You can't blame the process of networking. It's proven. It delivers. If you find you're not winning business or meeting the right people from your networking efforts, that's your fault. And now that you're fully prepared to walk into a room, let's focus on helping you execute.

The first step towards getting somewhere is to decide that you are not going to stay where you are.

J.P. Morgan

Part II
While you're there

The time has come to actually walk into a room. We're focused here on the face-to-face side of networking. Shaking hands, pressing the flesh, working the room, schmoozing – whatever you want to call it.

Of course, you know it's simply meeting new people, having conversations and building relationships. And it's all coachable. Remember, though, that like your networking strategy, there is no one definitive best way to execute. There are many ways to handle the networking dialogue, to work a room and make networking work. Your job is to find your way.

In this part, you're going to be walking in with a positive, expectant outlook. You'll be getting comfortable during those critical first two minutes. You'll be moving into groups and conversations, introducing yourself and making a good impression. You'll be directing conversations, asking good questions and uncovering opportunities. You'll be introducing others, working the room and moving around. It's fun, especially when you know what you're doing.

Everyone is in sales. There is not a point in your day when you don't have to convince someone you are worth their time.

Joe Maddalone

7. How do you enter a room with confidence?

Nothing sells like certainty. As far as networking goes, it's important that you look confident and assured, even if you don't feel like it. As you travel to a networking event, it's time to get your mind in gear. You can draw networking confidence from the following eight sources:

① **Familiarity.** Knowing what you're walking into makes you more confident. If it's a new venue or somewhere you've never been, aim to acquaint yourself with your surroundings as quickly as you can. *Familiarity breeds confidence.*

② **Skills.** How good are you? The more skilful or competent you are in a particular area, the more confident you'll be performing it. Milking a cow is less intimidating if you've done it a hundred times before. *Competence breeds confidence.*

③ **Precedents.** What happened last time? If you've done well in the past, that gives you confidence for the future. A good outcome, a good result, a favourable experience – all feed your confidence engine. Draw on history. *Precedents breed confidence.*

④ **Allies.** Who else is going that you know? If you have friends, colleagues or known connections in the room, you've always got somebody safe to talk to. You may know in advance that they'll be there or you might just see them when you walk in. *Allies breed confidence.*

5. **Objectives.** If you know why you're there, you're much more likely to succeed. Once you have a goal or objective you are more purposeful. Set yourself an outcome that is achievable for each event, such as swapping five business cards or having three interesting conversations. *Goals breed confidence.*

6. **Quick wins.** If you can get into a interesting conversation early, it will make you more confident for what is to come. A joke, a familiar face, a relaxing drink – all can put you at ease and make you feel better about being there. *Quick wins breed confidence.*

7. **Legitimacy.** Do you have a right to be there? Are you as good as everyone else there? If you feel worthy, then you should feel confident. Nobody there is better than you. You've been invited just like they have. Your presence is warranted so walk tall. *Legitimacy breeds confidence.*

8. **Motivation.** Why are you networking? What's your reason for doing it all? Profile? New business? Whatever it is, go back to your source. This will drive you forward and give you the faith to go for it. The end results, the new leads and referrals – all make you want to be there. *Motivation breeds confidence.*

Once your mind is right and you're confident about what you're walking into, it's show time. And, like any great performer or athlete, the first couple of minutes can set the tone for the whole experience.

Bossing the critical first two minutes

You want to make a confident entrance? We call this bossing, or taking charge of a situation. To do that, your first thoughts and actions are important. They set the tone for your whole networking experience. Confidence breeds confidence, so early successes play a vital role. Here is your six-point checklist to help you maximise your confidence and focus on the first two minutes of arriving:

1. **Check your attitude.** Confidence is key. People buy certainty. You've got to look like you: (a) want to be there; and (b) have a right to be there.

2. **Survey the room.** This helps if the room or venue is unfamiliar to you. You're looking for who is there and what is around you. Find out where everything is. Observe the room layout and check where things are – drinks, bar, food, buffet, toilets, cloakroom, registration table, welcome area. There may also be some interesting aspects of the room you might comment on in a conversation.

3. **Do the necessaries.** This means get the administrative stuff sorted. Book yourself in, grab your badge, meet the organisers – all of that stuff. You may even get a drink as you arrive, and a copy of the attendee list or something about what's coming up.

4. **Look for allies.** Have a look around – is there anyone else you know there? A friendly face helps to soothe the nerves, even if you don't talk to them.

5. **Look for targets.** Where will your first conversation come from? Look for open twos and threes and, of course, people on their own. These are sometimes called the

white-knuckle networkers – they're often terrified and standing on their own looking rather forlorn and lonely.

6 **Make an approach.** Go over and say hello, especially to those people on their own. You'll be very welcome and make an instant friend now they are no longer on their own. Plus, you're now in your first conversation, which means you're up and running.

8. How do you decide exactly who to talk to?

Introducing yourself to strangers

Good networkers are proactive. They don't stand in the corner of a room and wait for people to come to them. You've got to make your move and introduce yourself to people. Thankfully, there are steps to doing this – all small ones which break down the process to be less intimidating and more achievable. Here they are:

1. **Check your attitude.** People buy certainty, so draw your confidence from any of the suggestions on pages 31 and 32. A little swagger (without being too arrogant or over-confident) generally makes you a more attractive and compelling proposition.

2. **Find your target.** Identify who will be your first conversation. You're looking for people on their own and open twos and threes who look approachable. Stay away from the closed groups as these people are giving out a clear signal that, at least for the moment, they don't want to be interrupted.

3. **Plan your approach.** Unless there is a direct pathway to your target, you may need to think for a moment about

how you reach them. If they are in an opposite corner of the room, choose a route to them which is less crowded and easy to negotiate. You might be carrying a drink at this stage, so make it easy for yourself.

4 **Respect personal space.** Just before you get to your intended target, stop short. This is polite and respectful. Walking right up to somebody nose to nose is too intimidating and doesn't make a great first impression.

5 **Make eye contact.** Add a smile to this. It makes you warm, inviting and non-threatening. A lot has been written about making first impressions count. The best advice is to be relaxed, genuine and prepared.

6 **Ask a question.** The best chat-up lines and, indeed, networking lines are often questions. *Hi, do you mind if I join you? Can I join you? Hi, I'm Rob. Mind if I join you?* These are nice, easy opening lines which are really hard to say no to. Don't overcomplicate things. It's just a simple introduction to a new friend.

7 **Offer your hand.** It's expected that you'll shake hands in most networking situations. If you have been carrying a drink in your right hand, swap it over before approaching. Make sure your hand is dry. Not hot and sweaty. Not cold and clammy. Neither are conducive to a favourable first impression.

8 **Shake hands well.** People overcomplicate handshakes. Too strong? Too aggressive? Too limp? The best advice is to let them squeeze your hand first and match the pressure they use in return. If you are in any doubt as to whether your handshake is conducive to good relations, have a close friend check it out. Otherwise, nobody will ever tell you.

Congratulations! You're now into a conversation. You've done the hard work and things should get a lot easier from here. Of course, now you're in a conversation, you need to know how to handle it and what to say. This is the networking dialogue and it starts with small talk.

Feel shy at parties? Imagine everyone has an invisible sign hanging from their neck saying *make me feel important*.

Mary Kay Ash

9. What's the best way to make the first move?

Why is small talk important and what do people talk about?

Some people struggle with small talk, but this is what oils the wheels of big-business conversations. In fact, small talk can lead to big business. It's basically any conversational topics that are nothing to do with business. Typical topics include the weather, your journey to the event, where you live, your hobbies, what's happening in the news, sport and the actual venue or event you're attending.

Good small talkers look for things in common. Sometimes called 'me too' topics, you're aiming for something in common with the person you're talking to. People tend to relax with and like people who have similar tastes to themselves. Think about food, drink, room and venue (FDRV). Stick to what you can see, because you have these four things in common with everybody in the room.

If you want to be a little more sophisticated, here are seven of my favourite small-talk questions to relax people, open them up and get them talking:

1. *What brought you here?* This is a nice open question and gives you some insight into their reasons for being there.

2 *What are you looking to get from today?* This question gives you a feel for their objectives – who they want to meet and what they are looking to achieve.

3 *Have you been to this event before?* If they haven't, then they're new like you. If they have, you can tap into their event experience.

4 *Who invited you here today?* It's an easy question to answer, and gives you a feel for their objectives.

5 *Have you come a long way?* Most people like to talk about their journeys and transport. They might also open up about where they came from.

6 *Do you do much networking?* If they do, ask them where. If they don't, you can always invite them to another event.

7 *What do you do when you're not networking?* This gives people a lot of scope to answer about their job, their hobbies, their family or pretty much anything else.

People usually like talking about themselves, so when they answer, show an interest. Good conversationalists are as much interested as they are interesting. Resist the temptation to hog the conversation and make it all about you. Actually, this is why many introverts make good networkers. They talk less, listen more and allow others to do most of the talking by asking good questions.

How can you move the conversation forward on to business topics?

At some point, you'll be ready to move on from small talk to the business talk. This is usually signified by the question *What do you do?* This gives rise to your elevator pitch, which we will come on to soon. Once people ask you what you do, they're showing interest in your job, your role, your business, your industry, your products and services.

Business talk is the commercial end of networking. When it comes to networking, the business talk sets you up to talk about their challenges and plans. It gives you the platform to ask the ultimate networking question, which is *How's business going?*

If business is going well, then there are plans and projects in hand. Goals, dreams, visions. Expansion, acquisition, growth. Lending, investing, hiring. Training, development and changes in strategy. All of these represent opportunities for you and people you know to help and advise, to consult, coach and mentor. Ultimately, to sell.

If business is not going so well, then there are problems and pains. Challenges and issues. Consolidation, cut-backs and cost reductions. Lay-offs, changes in strategy and realignment of priorities. Once more, all of these represent opportunities for you and people you know to help and advise, to consult, coach and mentor. Ultimately, to sell.

Are you getting the idea? Whether times are good or bad, you have the opportunity to help. That may mean to sell or to refer others in to sell. Opportunities arise from moving people from the small talk to the meatier topics of business issues. Few people handle this well, largely because they don't understand the Conversation Carousel.

The Conversation Carousel

New business doesn't arrive out of thin air. You've got to put seeds in the ground and create opportunities. To do that, you've got to build relationships. Why? Because virtually all of the opportunities you create will come from relationships. You're in a people business. That's how it works.

It's different if you're paying for advertising or paid traffic to generate leads. Or growing your business from email marketing or social media. We're talking about networking here, which is a people-oriented activity. You're in the relationship business, so your leads, referrals, prospects and opportunities will come from people.

So how do you build these relationships that lead to opportunities? You have conversations. Good conversations. And to do that you ask questions. Good questions. So we have this formula for creating networking ROI:

Good questions = good conversations = good relationships = good opportunities = good business

The beauty of a carousel is that it keeps going around. So, when you're finally doing business with somebody, you can ask deeper, more intimate questions, which allows you to have higher-quality conversations. As a result, you build better relationships and create more opportunities. Opportunities to cross-sell, up-sell, refer others and generally increase your share of wallet. That's the realm of key account management – looking after your clients. Plus, it keeps them more loyal, highlights any vulnerabilities and protects them from the advances of your competitors.

Figure 2 The Conversation Carousel

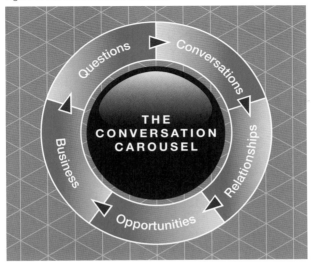

Here's another way of looking at the Conversation Carousel:

**More questions = more conversations = more relationships
= more opportunities = more business**

If you want more business over the next few months, go out there and start asking more (and better) questions. This will naturally lead to more (and better) conversations, which will undoubtedly lead to more (and better) relationships. Of course, this will generate much more (and better) opportunities, which ultimately gives you more (and better) business.

Networking is a relationship-building activity. Remember, it's talking and listening. Turning strangers into friends. Learning more about others and educating them about yourself. So let's explore some of those great questions that will end up bringing you the new business and sales you desire.

Class and charm is being able to make
people of all walks of life feel comfortable.

Susan RoAne

10. What are great networking questions to ask?

So you've gone to a networking event, you've made your approach and got into a few conversations. You've done the small talk and moved smoothly on to business talk. You're on your way to creating some opportunities or, at the very least, qualifying these prospects to see whether it benefits you both to keep talking.

Here are some of my favourite networking questions. You just need to ask a few to open people up beyond the small talk.

- What's your particular area of expertise?
- How did you get started?
- What do you like most about what you do?
- How many people do you work with?
- What's the biggest thing you're working on right now?
- What's the main thing (major focus) for you this year?
- What are your plans for the next 6–12 months?
- What's your biggest challenge at the moment?
- Who would be a good introduction for you?

- What kind of people are you looking to meet today?
- What's the best thing you've done recently for a client or customer?
- What do you do better or differently from the competition?
- How well do you compare to others who do what you do?

There are many more great networking questions, and you'll develop some for yourself, but you won't go wrong by weaving some of these questions into your networking conversations. They build trust and show you're genuinely taking an interest in people. If you can help them as a result of the answers you get, then great. If not, there's always the possibility that you can introduce them to someone who can help them. Referrals are the currency of relationships.

11. How do you properly move around and work a room?

Whether you call it schmoozing or working a room, you still have to move from one conversation to another. You still have to move in and out of groups, pass people on and introduce others. It's tricky, but it's doable. The Queen of Networking, Susan RoAne, was the first person to write about this in her book *How to Work a Room*. This title is now 25 years old and is the bible for mingling and mixing in a room full of strangers.

The essence of working a room is making the right approaches to the right people or groups, moving on when appropriate and introducing others when possible. It takes some practice to do it well – most people would rather stand in a corner and wait for the right people to come to them. Unfortunately, that's not an option for you, which is why the good networkers are proactive.

Here are a few tips for being more at ease in networking situations.

- **Respect personal space.** Don't get too close to people – it can be quite intimidating. If the room is noisy or crowded, you may need to be a bit closer. Otherwise, give people some space.

- **Smile.** Not constantly – that would be weird. But do keep smiling regularly, especially at key points in a conversation where a positive response is needed.

- **Maintain good eye contact.** Staring is off-putting, but frequent eye contact shows you are listening. Strike a balance. Too little eye contact gives the impression that you lack confidence or that you're not really interested in the conversation. Too much indicates that you are either weird or aggressive.

- **Have a good handshake.** As you've learned, your handshake has to be just right. A firm handshake demonstrates confidence and friendliness.

- **Introduce others well.** Use names of all parties if you can remember them. If possible, say something about the people you're introducing. *'Hi Jane, have you met Joe? He's the founder of XYZ. Jane is an expert in ABC…'* Alternatively, offer a hint of what you've just been talking about. *'Hey Tim, this is Julie. We were just speaking about what an incredible venue this is…'*.

The importance of remembering names

How many times have you met someone new and asked their name, and then a couple of minutes into the conversation you realise you've forgotten who you're speaking to? More often than is comfortable? It's very important to remember names. People feel you care about them if you make the effort to remember them.

Conversely, if you forget their name, they feel aggrieved. So, when they give their name for the first time, make your mind zero in on the name, so that you absorb it. Then, begin using it straight away. Your first reply should be, 'Tim, nice to meet you.' And then sprinkle their name through your conversation. Repeating it in this way will help you remember it.

The first step in remembering names is wanting to. Unless you care enough or feel it's important, you won't really commit. And it's not just their name that counts. If they mention the name of their partner, dog, football team, children, boss, then do everything you can to commit those to memory. It's valuable intelligence. It helps you stand out when you remember soft facts like this.

Your memory is a muscle. It can be trained or neglected. It works best with concentration, repetition and reinforcement. If you commit to improving even ten per cent with names, you will definitely build rapport faster, and build relationships more quickly. Set mini-goals, like remembering five names in a room. You'll soon find you can do 10 and then 20.

Cultivate a good attitude for remembering names. Saying you've 'got a bad memory' or you can 'never remember names' is negative. Such thinking will not serve your networking efforts. If you were challenged to remember 50 names at a networking event for a prize of £50,000, I'm sure you'd be focused. Names are vital, so make every effort to ask for them, remember them and, most importantly, use them.

Making a good first impression

First impressions really do matter. Experts say it takes you just 30 to 90 seconds to assess a new person. First impressions also set pretty quickly, so you don't have long to make a good impression. This means you need to be friendly, relaxed and yet enthusiastic. Here are some tips to make a better first impression when you meet new people:

- **Remember and use names.** You've seen how vital names can be. Using somebody's name in the first few seconds of meeting them shows you care and are giving them attention.

- **Stay focused.** Concentrate while people are talking. Minds wander and eyes get distracted. Listen carefully to what your conversation partner is saying. Don't let your mind wander. If you listen well to people's comments and answers to your questions, you'll know what to say to keep the ball rolling. You'll also avoid the embarrassment of misunderstanding what they have said and so giving a stupid reply.

- **Ask good questions.** Good conversationalists keep conversations moving and interesting. Their primary weapon is asking good questions. Arm yourself with a few and you'll never be short of an engaging conversation.

- **Show genuine interest.** Aim to be more interested than interesting. Some people talk about themselves a lot. They rarely ask about you or, if they do, they cut your answer short and move the conversation back to themselves again. Not you.

- **Be enthusiastic.** Try to appear positive and passionate. Boring people make little networking impact. Dial up enthusiasm by ten per cent above your natural level. If you're happy to be there and keen to do business, let it show.

- **Disengage well.** When you know how to get away properly, people appreciate it. If you feel you've been talking to the same person too long, they'll probably feel the same. Moving on politely always creates a favourable first impression. Here are a few useful disengagement scripts you could use or adapt: 'It's been nice meeting you; perhaps I'll see you later on?', 'Well, better get some more networking done;

it's been good to meet you', 'I've enjoyed meeting you; I wish you luck with the rest of your networking', 'Well thanks for a nice conversation; I'd better move around and meet some more people'.

As well as first impressions counting, first impressions also last. People form opinions quickly, so in the short networking time you are together, do all you can to make those precious seconds count. Even if you don't care too much what a certain person thinks of you, they've got friends in high places. And friends talk. So protect your reputation and make your first impressions good ones.

Crafting your elevator pitch

Your answer to the 'What do you do?' question is a critical moment in your networking conversation. This is your elevator pitch. Imagine getting into an elevator with your top prospect and they ask you what you do. What would you reply that would make them want to leave with your business card?

You're going to get asked what you do every time you go networking. Every time you meet a stranger. You need to prepare an answer that makes people remember you and what you do, and tells them how you can help them. This is no time to be spontaneous, or you could mess up your greatest opportunity to win future business.

If you just give your job title, you will probably become immediately forgettable. Saying you're an accountant or a lawyer or in banking allows your conversation partner to put you in that box with all the other people who do that job. You don't want to be in that box. When people buy Black & Decker, they're not buying quarter-inch drills but quarter-inch holes. The marketeers got this right: they're not selling drills, but holes.

Get rid of the polite, bland introductions that get in the way of a great pitch. Do your homework by knowing your market and yourself. Ask yourself these questions:

- Who do you want to sell to?
- What are the key strengths of your offering?
- What adjectives best describe them?
- What do you want your audience to know?
- How is your offering better than your competition's?

Once you have these answers, you can use the following six questions to help you craft your perfect networking introduction:

1. Who are you?

2. Who is your target audience or ideal prospect?

3. What are you offering?

4. What problems can you solve?

5. What is your unique benefit to your customers or clients?

6. What would you like your audience to do now?

Crafting your elevator pitch takes a bit of thinking through. It needs preparing and practising. Only then will you deliver it properly. You may need a few different versions depending on how long you have and who your audience is. The best net-workers are prepared. They also ask a few questions of their audience before having to give their elevator pitch. That way, when the time comes, they can give a more relevant, specific answer.

12. What do you look for in a networking conversation?

You want to help people. You want to raise your profile and build your business. You want people to help you. You should be looking for that 'let's do business' revelation! This is the moment when you feel enough of a connection to swap business cards. Good networkers are trained to recognise the moment of truth or the 'a-ha' moment.

So what kinds of things could you be looking for in a networking situation that might create an opportunity for this to happen? Here are some things to ask about and look for when you're talking to somebody face to face. Any of these will give you an 'in' for your networking follow-up.

- **Plans and projects**. What plans have they got? If they are looking to grow, you might be able to help them, or know somebody who can. Plans = opportunities.

- **Problems and pain**. What problems are they having? Problems are always opportunities to help, sell or refer. They say money follows pain, so look out for what challenges people are having.

- **Social media**. What online networking channels are they active on? If you know you can find them online, this puts much less pressure on you trying to find out all about them and get their business card. In such situations, when you know someone is online, you should focus more on the small talk to build the trust.

- **No previous experience**. Ask people if they do much networking. If they don't, you're in a great position to really help them by introducing them to a few people there and showing them the ropes. They'll really appreciate it. Remember, you were new at this game once.

- **Previous experience**. If they've done a lot of networking, ask where else they go. You might uncover some new events, groups or clubs. You might also learn where to avoid.

- **Current network**. Where is their network strong? Who else do they know? These are important things to look out for. What names or sectors do they drop into the conversation? Who are their prospects, clients or customers?

- **Right person**. Let's say you're chatting to a good prospect. Is it actually them you should be following up with? If not, there's no harm in asking who might be the person you should call.

- **Key target**. In Chapter 15, you'll find a list of five types of people you should (and shouldn't) be looking to engage with and follow through on after networking with them. Keep a lookout for such people – they are gold dust.

- **Insight**. Any industry knowledge, market insight, local opportunities, deals or openings… you can learn a lot from your networking with some good questioning and some good listening.

There will be other things to look out for. Any of these good reasons should get your networking antenna twitching. Be open, be sensitive, be responsive, be curious and be bold. These nuggets you collect at the 'let's do business' moment will help you position the follow-up call. People will be more open to you following up your networking encounter if you've got a good reason for doing so!

Key takeaways

- If you feel good walking into a room full of strangers, you're not normal.

- Introducing yourself to strangers is a simple step-by-step approach. Once conquered, you can use it time and time again to make a good first impression.

- Great business comes from opportunities, which come from relationships, which come from conversations, which come from questions. This is the Conversation Carousel.

- Have a few good small-talk and business-talk networking questions memorised so you can always keep the conversation going.

- Remembering names and making a good first impression are vital networking skills that everyone can improve on.

- Your elevator pitch answers 'What do you do?' in a way that makes you memorable, different and useful.

- Listen well and always be on the lookout for opportunities to help, sell, refer or introduce when you're talking to people.

You network to help others and, in doing so, you help yourself. Look for ways to solve problems, address challenges, relieve pain and contribute to business success. See if you can save people time, money or effort, or perhaps increase their skills and knowledge. Once you've had the conversations and perhaps uncovered some opportunities, you just have to get their card and follow up. That comes next.

Part III
After you've been

Following up means making the most of those networking contacts you've met. The hard work is done in carving out the opportunity and positioning yourself well to start a business relationship. Now you've got to keep it going. The problem arises when you consider how unusual it would be for strangers you meet networking to have an exact need for exactly what you offer at that exact time. It rarely happens and, without that tangible opportunity to do immediate business, few follow up.

From my experience, fewer than ten per cent of the prospects you meet networking will need what you do and have the budget to pay for it at the exact moment you meet them. The other 90 per cent will be in the market for your products and services at some unspecified point in the future. Seeds need to be sown for long-term relationships, because the need will arise months and perhaps years down the line.

The successful networking follow-up is all about helping you make the most of those hot contacts you meet when you are networking. There is no excuse not to keep in touch with people these days. It's the biggest networking crime to go to one meeting or have one conversation and just leave it at that. If you don't follow up on the contacts you make at networking events, it's like you never went.

Great works are performed not by strength
but by perseverance.

Samuel Johnson

13. Why is it vital to follow up your networking?

You've maybe been guilty in the past of not following through on your networking. Yet, it's the only way to turn those business cards into sales and make your networking count. But it doesn't happen instantly. It's a shame and a waste to commit that precious time to going out there, meeting people, making connections and swapping cards, only to fail to follow it up.

Profitable networking as a process is more than an event. It begins with a conversation and features lots more conversations across various media over an undefined period of time. Stories abound of people who have made a networking connection, only for it to take years for the sale to land. Of course, you can often accelerate the buying cycle with a systematic follow-up and keep-in-touch regime. If you get lucky and land a deal or referral without any follow-up, that's the exception rather than the norm.

By playing a long-term game and keeping in touch, you're more likely to be called when they need you. Your prospect will probably have existing advisors, providers or suppliers in place. They may already have a go-to source for what you do.

But things change, suppliers change, circumstances change, budgets change, strategies change. So you still might get a shot at pitching for their business, to be in prime position when things change. Then you become the spare wheel when they get a puncture. You're next in line. When their strategy or game plan changes, you're first off the substitutes bench.

The networking follow-up can be paralysing. You may fear rejection and perhaps don't quite know how to follow up. You're sometimes more comfortable going out to a fresh networking event and meeting more new people, but the chances are you won't follow up with them either. These are the key reasons why you should follow up your networking:

- **Because you said you would.** You did say you'd follow up with them, didn't you? You did indicate that it would be good for you to keep in touch, right? So not doing so is breaking a promise. If you promised to call, how bad will it look if you don't?

- **You might damage your reputation.** By not calling, you may show yourself to be uncaring or disorganised. Neither is good for your reputation.

- **It makes you stand out.** Most people don't follow up. You're not most people. That's why you are going to follow up and make yourself memorable.

- **It shows you are professional.** If they see that you are diligent with your networking follow-up, they'll be more likely to refer you and do business with you.

- **You hold back your competitors.** If you neglect to call, some of your competitors might. You don't want them stepping into your shoes and stealing those opportunities you've worked hard to create while networking.

- **It keeps you front of mind.** If you are networking with the right people, then hopefully they will need you, can help you or might refer you at some point in the future. Your follow-up increases the chances that they will turn to you when they need what you do at that moment in time.

- **You might lose out.** Recognise that if you don't make the call, you may lose a profitable new customer or client. Worse, you may let a great referral partner slip through your fingers – someone who could introduce you to several new clients.

- **It builds trust in you as a person.** Showing up is not enough. You have to build on that visibility with credibility. That's why you need to follow up. By doing what you say you will do, you build trust and relationship capital.

- **You want the business.** Or the referral. Or the alliance. Or the investment. Whatever you're after, if you don't follow up, you're probably not going to get it.

- **It's worth it financially.** Consider how much you might lose by not making the call. If they end up buying from you, consider the lifetime value of that contact or potential client. More than buying or referring once, they might stay with you for years. This follow-up conversation isn't a 'nothing' call. It could be worth thousands to you.

- **You can't afford not to.** Let's add this up. You probably spent two or three hours at the networking event. Plus your travel to and from the event. Plus any membership fees, costs for petrol, food and drink. That's a lot of wasted time and money if you don't get something from it.

- **It avoids any regret or uncertainty.** Remember that if you don't call, you'll never know what might have happened. You'll never know what business you could have won. You won't ever have to worry about all the what-ifs if you follow up your networking.

13. Why is it vital to follow up your networking?

You network to make money, not spend money. Unfortunately, it sometimes seems the other way around. You cannot afford to waste valuable time, money and effort by not following up. That's why the stuff you do after you've been networking is the most important of all.

14. What stops you from following up?

What stops you doing that follow-up call or message when you know you should? Why do you hesitate? Here are some of the most common reasons why you don't do the networking follow-up, and suggestions for how to overcome them:

- **You lose their card.** Sounds crazy, but many people do it. Have a system with bags, handbags, purses, pockets and wallets.

- **You are really disorganised.** What does your desk look like? If it's a mess, you could be sabotaging your chances of making a disciplined and effective follow-up.

- **You worry about how they will respond.** Will they remember you? Will they want to talk to you? Remember, this is just a continuation of the conversation you were having face to face just a few short days ago.

- **You fear showing desperation.** It's okay to feel a little scared, but you can't let them see that. There are loads of mind games and positive mental attitude exercises you can try, but desperation isn't referable or attractive!

- **You forget.** It might just slip your mind to put the call in your diary. There's being disorganised, then there's plain forgetfulness. There's no excuse for this, but people do it.

- **You fear rejection.** If you give those negative networking demons a foothold in your brain, you'll never turn your business cards into sales and your contacts into contracts. The networking follow-up is as much in the mind as anywhere else; if you're good at what you do and your networking contact would benefit from knowing you, then you should have every confidence in making that call or sending that email.

- **You feel pushy.** You may be conscious of pushing too hard, but actually few people cross this line. They expect you to follow up. You said you would and you are. That's just commitment – doing what you said you'd do! As long as you're not pestering them, your follow-up is within acceptable limits.

- **You are too busy.** Things come up. It's easy for your networking follow-ups to get swallowed in the minutiae of your day. Life is busy. There's so much to do. You've got to prioritise your networking follow-up just like you would other vital areas of business. You might have the best of intentions, but your lack of time management and priorities is not helping you fulfil them.

The fortune is in the follow-up. You can be fantastic working the room. You can be the life and soul of the party. You might be the funniest, most engaging person on the planet. But, if you cannot or will not follow up, it's almost impossible to be successful in business. Make it your goal to develop both skill sets of successful networking. Overcome your networking inhibitions and get that networking follow-up done.

15. How do you decide who to follow up with?

It's not what you know, it's who you know and who knows you. But who exactly are the right people to know? You meet all kinds of people when networking. Some are useful and interesting. Some are useless and boring. Some want to sell to you and others you want to sell to. Some need you more than you need them. Some don't care about you as much as you care about them. Some you can really help but they can't help you. Some are really well placed to aid your cause, but you're not in a position to help them back.

The good networkers know exactly who to engage with and follow up with. You don't want to follow up with everyone, and they don't want you to either. You just have to be a little discerning with your choices. There are many kinds of people you might meet at a business-related event or even online that you should definitely follow up and keep in touch with. Here are some of the main ones if you've got a sales or business-development angle to your role.

1. **Hot prospects.** People in your target market who need what you do right now. If they are the purse-holder or decision maker, even better. Don't let these people slip through your fingers. Follow up and weave them into your sales process – your networking has generated a lead.

2 **Potential prospects.** People who might need what you do in the future. The timing might not be right, or they are in a sector or area you're thinking of moving into. They will fill your sales pipeline for the future.

3 **Interesting unknowns.** This is the name I give to networking contacts you are curious about and need to find out more about. They could be a valuable addition to your network. You just don't know yet, hence the reason to follow up and either build the relationship or, as the police would say, 'eliminate them from your enquiries'.

4 **Influencers.** These VIPs have influence, reach, kudos and leverage. They get things done and make things happen. They may be famous or prestigious. They may be a thought leader, an innovator or a player. Good networkers know how to make friends with top influencers.

5 **Referral sources.** People who can introduce you to your target market. They will probably be supplying that market already, but with a non-competing product or service. If you can refer them to your clients, you've got a very powerful referral partnership in the making.

This list is not exhaustive, but might give you better perspective when you meet people when out networking. You'll be able to make a much more informed decision about whether or not you should get their card and stay in touch. This wisdom and discernment in knowing where and when to spend your time is the difference between good and great networkers.

People you should not follow up after networking

One of the qualities that separates the great networkers from the average ones is discerning which contacts to follow up on and which ones to leave alone. You have enough to do already without going on wild goose chases, following futile connections and wasting precious time on the wrong people. Here are five types of people who you might want to think twice about before following up with after a networking encounter:

1. **People who just want to sell to you.** Unless you're buying, showing these kinds of people any interest will be a distraction.

2. **Nice people.** Beware of these people. Just because they're nice doesn't mean they should be followed up. Nice on its own isn't a strong enough reason to sustain the relationship, unless you're just lonely and looking for friends. Look for a tangible reason to meet up and stay in touch. If they're a nice person too, then that's a bonus!

3. **Rude people.** If you have the choice, wouldn't you rather do business with friendly people? If at all possible, stay away from the rude people. Life is too short.

4. **Time wasters.** These are people who promise much but deliver little. You should be able to spot the freeloaders and tyre-kickers who are just killing time. They may pretend that they're interested in you and what you do, but they are not. They may be trying to chat you up for free advice or consultancy. They may just be using you to benchmark their existing suppliers. They could just be lonely. Good networkers are friendly, but they can also be ruthless. If you feel someone is fishing for free, ask them a few rigorous questions around timescales, budgets, business problems and current providers to establish their true intentions.

5. **Card sharks.** These are people who just make it their business to collect as many business cards as possible. It's sometimes a game to them. They're not really interested

in doing business, but they might string you along a merry dance if you become too involved.

All relationships are a factor of time spent on, around and with people, but there is an 'opportunity cost'. If you spend 20 minutes on one person, you can't spend those 20 minutes on another person. You must be discerning and even ruthless in deciding who you will spend time with and who you will follow up on. This is why it's critical to learn from your face-to-face networking encounter or somebody's online profile. When you are armed with the right information, you can make a better decision about who to follow up and who to leave alone.

16. How do you do an effective follow-up?

In the past, the networking follow-up would consist solely of a phone call and perhaps a follow-up meeting. As technology increased, we started using faxes and emails. Today, follow-up is even more varied and sophisticated. There are many different channels of communication through which you can follow up and keep in touch with your networking contacts. You don't need to master them all, but it would be good to conquer a few.

Remember, it's not just about you and your preferred communication methods. It's less good sending emails to someone who prefers talking on the phone, or posting messages on Twitter and Facebook if people would rather meet face to face. So, if you are planning to stay in touch, take a little time to establish how they stay connected to the network and which channels they prefer. Here are some great methods of communication you can use to connect with your networking contacts after the initial conversation:

- **Social media** (Twitter, Facebook and others). It's hard to escape the many online social networking channels that are available today. As one CEO of a global media company told me once, 'We have to maintain a presence using social media, because that's where our customers and prospects live.'

- **LinkedIn.** This is the world's largest professional business directory, and one you really should be on if you're serious about business. Ninety-nine per cent of the people you meet networking should now be on LinkedIn, so it's a perfect way to stay in contact and build a relationship.

- **Phone.** This is still one of the best business-development and relationship-building tools available. It's quick, it's two-way and it gives you the opportunity to be engaging, passionate, dynamic, informative and responsive.

- **Email.** This is now the most popular method of following up networking. It's quick, timely and informative. It's also easy to ignore or delete. Email is also good to use in conjunction with other follow-up strategies – a blended approach can hit lots of bases.

- **Face to face.** This is the most time-consuming but often the most constructive way to follow up your networking, particularly with a prospect. Whether it's a lunch, a cup of coffee, a scheduled one-to-one meeting, simply dropping by at their office or inviting them to join you at an upcoming networking event, the face-to-face follow-up is a high-impact strategy for your very best networking contacts.

- **Text message.** Sometimes a quick text follow-up can hit the mark as a valuable way of keeping the relationship going. I use this one a lot straight after a networking event – it lands almost immediately and is a nice touch point to prepare the ground for your next follow-up.

- **Skype call or chat.** Skype is becoming an increasingly popular means of communication. It has a visual and audio element as well as the capacity to instantly chat through written words. If you check out people's email signatures, you'll find that many are beginning to have their Skype address featured, along with their phone and email details. If it's there, why not use it?

- **Post.** Everyone loves to get mail. Handwritten notes are ideal and certainly portray your personality and desire to invest the time in fostering a relationship. You should strongly consider this as a first-choice contact mechanism for your highest priority contacts. It takes time, but it really stands out.

Remember your follow-up choice of communication is not about you. This is about them and the way they like to communicate. The good networkers do a little digging to find out how their contacts like to stay in touch. Then they use those methods to maintain the connection.

How and when do you follow up your networking?

People are different. We all like different things. In deciding how to build on your initial networking conversation, consider the following, all of which will turn your cards and contacts into customers and clients.

- **Their needs.** What did they say they wanted? What were their challenges and problems? Be aware of their needs and you'll find a more receptive audience.

- **Their timing.** How urgent is it that you follow up quickly? Did they reveal anything about what's going on in their business or life right now? If it's an accounting year end, if they're on the verge of winning or losing a big contract, if they've got a daughter starting college or a son getting married – you've got a lot of 'noise' to get through.

- **The conversational topics.** What did you talk about? If it was mostly social and personal stuff, then there's less need for an urgent follow-up. If it was a more commercial conversation, perhaps even with a potential prospect, then it's wise to strike quickly and decisively.

- **How memorable you are.** How much will they remember the conversation? How much will they remember you? What did you do to stand out? If there was good chemistry and you got along, then you can follow up any time. The less memorable you are, the more you need to strike quickly.

- **Your diary.** How busy are you? Most people don't leave time to follow up their networking. If you have a busy few days after an event, you're not in a great position to follow up quickly. Try to block out some calendar time.

- **Your urgency.** How much do you want the business? How much do you *need* to make that sale, get that referral or close that contact?

- **Your systems.** What processes, procedures and systems do you have in place to ensure you do what you need to do? A CRM system or similar is vital. A good diary or calendar system is important. Good support from staff, secretaries or PAs can be crucial. Your to-do lists and memory systems will all serve you or fail you in your attempts to turn cards into contracts.

If you're going to turn your business networking into business and sales, follow up often and follow through well. You don't really get paid to network. In fact, networking costs you a lot of money, time and effort. Instead, you probably get paid on the results of your networking. Following up is the difference between getting that job or not, in securing that sale or not, in winning that new client or not.

How to get organised for following up networking

Your follow-up starts before you walk in the door of any business event. Many amateur networkers think that following up just means getting someone's business card and entering their contact information into a database. That's the end, not the start of a relationship.

The follow-up creates another opportunity to interact. Otherwise, relationships can't develop. It's good business to nurture your professional contacts so they develop into something more. Those who don't follow up their networking are often the same people who say networking doesn't work. Networking does work if you're prepared and organised to carry out the right follow-up activities. Here are seven key tips for getting more organised:

1. **Set goals or targets for following up.** You can't hit what you can't see. Just like sales targets, be focused on hitting your follow-up objectives. For yourself, if not for anyone else.

2. **Network less.** This might sound strange, but be more strategic with your networking so you actually do less of it. As a result, you'll have fewer people to follow up, so you can focus more on spending time developing existing relationships. More time means you can communicate more often, stay relevant and stay recent.

3. **Run a good CRM system.** CRM is a contact management system. Whatever you use for email is simply an address book and is not sophisticated in managing your contacts, tracking and creating follow-up reminders and storing relevant information. There are many CRM systems out there.

(4) Transfer business card details. In the olden days, you'd have boxes of business cards. It's actually a really inefficient way to manage your contacts. Get the information into your CRM system – only keep a small number of 'high touch' cards so you don't clutter too much.

(5) Use reminders and to-do lists. Set reminders through your CRM to call or follow up certain people at certain times. Otherwise, you'll get overwhelmed by how much you have to remember.

(6) Schedule follow-up time. Too many amateur networkers squeeze their networking into busy days and have no time for following up before the next event comes around. Set aside time to do any research, go through your cards, make those calls and implement your follow-up contact strategies.

(7) Categorise your follow-ups. A 'hot lead' or a 'perfect fit' is more urgent than a lukewarm contact. Categorising your networking contacts into an A, B or C-type system will help you prioritise which ones to follow up with first, and which not at all.

Your networking follow-up should be a critical marketing skill. You should treat it with at least the same importance as you do your actual networking. Whether you call it personal development, personal marketing, reputation management, lead generation or referral marketing skill development, the networking follow-up is a crucial part of the mix.

Great things to follow up with after a networking event

Networking is a people game. It kickstarts connections and builds your sales pipeline. If you're struggling with what to follow up with, try to add value and help people. They may buy or refer you at some point, but giving first is a great start. Here are six great follow-up ideas:

1. Send something useful by post. A book or other gift is nice. The more relevant, the better.

2. Connect to them on social media. If they are active on LinkedIn, Twitter or Facebook, give them a like, share or shout-out.

3. Share a resource. Email them a valuable website, ebook, article or blog.

4. Make an introduction. Could you introduce them to an investor, potential partner, professional advisor, coach, potential employee or even a prospect by way of a referral?

5. Give them a testimonial. Perhaps a LinkedIn recommendation or endorsement. If you feel comfortable and you know them enough, this is high value.

6. Invite them to something. You both met at a networking event, so could you invite them to an upcoming business event?

Anything you can do to make people feel good, feel special, feel cared for, feel memorable, feel valued or feel they matter is a massively worthwhile investment in your networking contacts.

Great tips for following up your networking online

One of the easiest touch points to make in your networking follow-up is an online connection. Most people are now on LinkedIn, so it's an easy and early 'win' to connect to them. LinkedIn allows you to see who they are connected to. Try a simple, 'It was great to meet you at the XYZ event. Let's connect on LinkedIn also.' Here are some great tips for connecting online as part of your networking follow-up:

- **Keep your profiles updated**. If you are on any online networks, ensure you have a photo uploaded on each profile. Please make sure it's a professional photo and not one of you partying!

- **Personalise your messages**. Online networks such as LinkedIn provide standard connection requests. Don't use these. Add a customised message which shows you've made the effort to be personal and relevant. The person is much more likely to say yes to your request to connect if you do this.

- **Integrate your online and offline worlds**. You should be making time to network on platforms such as LinkedIn and, to a lesser extent, Twitter and Facebook. You can often be more productive spending one hour a week on LinkedIn than three hours at a face-to face networking event. The best way is to balance them both.

- **Connect before you meet**. If you know who is going to a networking event beforehand, a clever way to enhance the relationship is to connect online before you meet. Occasionally, you will be able to ask the event organisers, meeting planners and hosts to supply delegate lists and guest lists ahead of time.

- **Find out if they are active online**. Ask them if they network online and where. Twitter, Facebook and LinkedIn are common and acceptable. It's another great way to keep the conversation going.

Once connected on LinkedIn or other online networking channels, a good read of their profile may identify other opportunities and topics to address in your follow-up. With all these online channels at your disposal, there is no excuse for the savvy networker to lose out on business. Just recognise that networking is a prospecting tool that kickstarts relationships and keeps your pipeline full.

Key takeaways

You've been networking and you come back with a handful of business cards. Is your job done? Sure, you've been networking, but now is where the hard work starts. Too many people spend valuable time networking, only to return to the office, put the collected business cards on their desk, turn to their inbox and say, 'Right, where was I?'

- All good networkers know the importance of the networking follow-up. An appropriate and sincere follow-up will ultimately lead to meaningful and fruitful relationships.

- You've just got to look for or create the right openings and follow them through. Often the hard work is done while you're networking by steering the conversation towards what you need to know.

- Networking is not a one-night stand. It's a long-term relationship. Conversion and ROI take time, so be patient.

- People won't give you business immediately, which is why you need to follow up and keep in touch.

- There are many gremlins, fears and obstacles that get in the way of following up. Recognise and conquer.

- Stay open to who you meet networking. Prospects are good. Introducers are also good.

- Networking takes up precious time. It makes sense to network with and follow up a few select people.

- The phone is good to follow up with, but there are now many other methods to stay connected, especially with online platforms and social media.

- Turning cards into contracts means getting organised and disciplined with your follow-up.

Your networking journey starts here

Many networkers trust to luck. You hope you'll meet lots of hot prospects who are ready to buy what you do or offer. Unfortunately, this is not the case. You must be able to do the sexy working the room stuff *and* the boring following-up stuff. That's what turns business cards into clients and conversations into contracts.

The people who rise to the top of any field or company are often not the most knowledgeable, the most technical, the most gifted, the most qualified or even the best. The people for whom most success is reserved are those who build the best relationships, make the most powerful connections, cultivate the key contacts and bring in the most business.

As a result of reading this *Authority Guide to Networking for Business Growth*, you are already a much more confident and effective networker. You've gained a complete grounding in what it takes to make networking work. Few people take this step, which is why you'll have the edge when it comes to generating more business from your networking efforts.

Going forward, keep your networking skills sharp, your mind open and your attitude positive. A world of opportunity, fun, wealth and recognition awaits you. Enjoy the journey, because who knows what lies on the other side of a good handshake and a courageous hello?

Happy networking!

About the author

Rob Brown is founder and CEO of the Networking Coaching Academy and the most recommended networking expert in the world, according to LinkedIn. He has trained and coached thousands of professionals to build their reputation and become confident, successful business networkers.

He is author of the hardback book *Build Your Reputation: Grow your personal brand for career and business success* (Wiley, 2016). A featured TED speaker, his talk 'The Personal Brand of You' has already had 50,000 views.

Rob's areas of expertise cover business networking, referrals, influence, trust, likeability, personal branding and reputation. He has worked with clients such as RBS, HSBC, Lloyds, IoD, GE, FSB, various Chambers of Commerce and a range of professional accounting, legal, finance and recruitment firms.

After brain surgery in 2016, Rob recalibrated his business to do less keynote speaking and travelling. He now works almost exclusively delivering in-house Business Development Academies for large law and accounting firms.

Rob lives in Nottingham with his wife, Amanda, and two daughters, Georgia and Madison. He has a black belt in kickboxing and does boot-camps (outdoor circuit training) three times a week to stay in shape.

He plays four musical instruments moderately well. He has even recorded an album of his own songs. His favourite gadgets are his bread machine, his Kindle and his Android phone.

His favourite authors are Lee Child and Robin Hobb, and his favourite 'very middle of the road' musical favourites are Lighthouse Family, Van Morrison, George Michael and the Carpenters.

Rob is a committed Christian and small-time philanthropist who is much involved in his local church. An enthusiastic chess and backgammon hustler, he loves eating milk chocolate, watching movies and listening to comedians.

Rob's five core values are family, faith, health, learning and optimism. He is ENTJ on Myers Briggs, predominantly D on DISC and a Creator-Star-Mechanic profile on Wealth Dynamics.

Travel wise, Rob has visited many countries as a speaker and regular traveller, and has lived in Hong Kong and the USA. He has visited every US state apart from two – perhaps you can guess which two.

Other Authority Guides

The Authority Guide to
Trusted Selling:
Building stronger, deeper, more profitable
relationships with your customers to
create lifetime loyalty

Paul Avins

Do you want to build more profitable relationships with your customers?

In today's volatile world sales professionals must know how to build trust in their company, their products and ultimately themselves in order to win the business. In this *Authority Guide*, sales coach Paul Avins shares his proven 4-step system to help you contact, connect and convert more customers with less effort and no pressure.

THE
AUTHORITY
GUIDES

We hope that you've enjoyed reading this *Authority Guide*. Titles in this series are designed to offer highly practical and easily-accessible advice on a range of business, leadership and management issues.

We're always looking for new authors. If you're an expert in your field and are interested in working with us, we'd be delighted to hear from you. Please contact us at commissioning@suerichardson.co.uk and tell us about your idea for an *Authority Guide*.